BRETT FAVRE, PAUL HORNUNG, JIM TAYLOR, DON HUTSON, G SHARPE, PAUL COFFMAN, FORREST GREGG, CAL HUBBARD, JERRY KRAMER, MIKE MICHALSKE, JIM RINGO, WILLIE DAVIS, REGGIE WHITE, RYAN PICKETT, HENRY JORDAN, RAY NITSCHKE, JOHN ANDERSON, DAVE ROBINSON, HERB ADDERLEY, CHARLES

THE STORY OF THE GREEN BAY PACKERS

WOODSON, WILLIE WOOD, LEROY BUTLER, RYAN LONGWELL, CRAIG HENTRICH, AL CARMICHAEL, BRETT FAVRE, PAUL HORNUNG, JIM TAYLOR, DON HUTSON, STERLING SHARPE, PAUL COFFMAN, FORREST

THE STORY OF THE
GREEN BAY
PACKERS

BY JIM WHITING

CREATIVE EDUCATION / CREATIVE PAPERBACKS

PUBLISHED BY CREATIVE EDUCATION AND CREATIVE PAPERBACKS
P.O. BOX 227, MANKATO, MINNESOTA 56002
CREATIVE EDUCATION AND CREATIVE PAPERBACKS ARE IMPRINTS OF THE
CREATIVE COMPANY
WWW.THECREATIVECOMPANY.US

DESIGN AND PRODUCTION BY BLUE DESIGN (WWW.BLUEDES.COM)
ART DIRECTION BY RITA MARSHALL
PRINTED IN CHINA

PHOTOGRAPHS BY GETTY IMAGES (LEE BALTERMAN/SI, JAMES V. BIEVER,
VERNON BIEVER/NFL, MATT CAMPBELL/AFP, KEVIN CASEY, TOM DAHLIN,
JONATHAN DANIEL, DAVID DRAPKIN, ELSA, JAMES FLORES/NFL, FOCUS
ON SPORT, ANDY HAYT, STREETER LECKA, AL MESSERSCHMIDT, RONALD C.
MODRA/SPORTS IMAGERY, DARRYL NORENBERG/NFL, PRO FOOTBALL HALL OF
FAME, PRO FOOTBALL HALL OF FAME/NFL, ART RICKERBY/TIME & LIFE
PICTURES, DAVID STLUKA, JOHN ZICH/AFP), NEWSCOM (ROBIN ALAM/ICON
SPORTSWIRE 164, AL GOLUB/ZUMA PRESS, LOUIS LOPEZ/CAL SPORT MEDIA)

NAMES: WHITING, JIM, AUTHOR.
TITLE: THE STORY OF THE GREEN BAY PACKERS / JIM WHITING.
SERIES: NFL TODAY.
INCLUDES INDEX.
SUMMARY: THIS HIGH-INTEREST HISTORY OF THE NATIONAL FOOTBALL
LEAGUE'S GREEN BAY PACKERS HIGHLIGHTS MEMORABLE GAMES, SUMMARIZES
SEASONAL TRIUMPHS AND DEFEATS, AND FEATURES STANDOUT PLAYERS SUCH
AS AARON RODGERS.
IDENTIFIERS: LCCN 2018059126 / ISBN 978-1-64026-141-9 (HARDCOVER) / ISBN
978-1-62832-704-5 (PBK) / ISBN 978-1-64000-259-3 (EBOOK)
SUBJECTS: LCSH: GREEN BAY PACKERS (FOOTBALL TEAM)—HISTORY—JUVENILE
LITERATURE. / GREEN BAY PACKERS (FOOTBALL TEAM)—HISTORY.
CLASSIFICATION: LCC GV956.G7 W55 2019 / DDC 796.332/640977561—DC23

FIRST EDITION HC 9 8 7 6 5 4 3 2 1
FIRST EDITION PBK 9 8 7 6 5 4 3 2 1

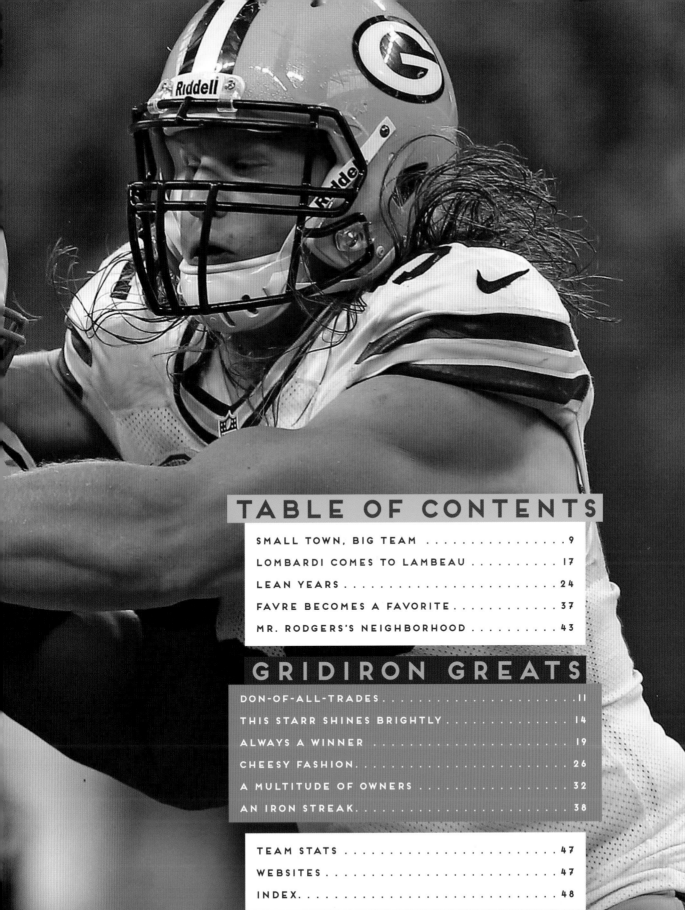

TABLE OF CONTENTS

GRIDIRON GREATS

SMALL TOWN, BIG TEAM

Curly Lambeau loved football. He played for the University of Notre Dame in 1918. After the season, Lambeau developed severe tonsillitis. He returned to his hometown of Green Bay, Wisconsin, and took a job at the Indian Packing Company. Lambeau and George Calhoun, editor of the *Green Bay Press-Gazette*, wanted to start a football team. First, they recruited players. Then, they asked Lambeau's employer to provide funding for equipment and uniforms. They called the team the Packers. This name recognized the company's support. It also reflected the importance of the meat packing industry in Green Bay. The Packers began playing in the fall of 1919.

GREEN BAY PACKERS

At that time, players worked full-time jobs. They squeezed in football practice when they could. "The men reporting regularly for the workouts will be given the first chance in the games," the newspaper noted. Lambeau and Calhoun had put together a powerhouse. In its first 10 games against Wisconsin and Upper Michigan rivals, the team scored 532 points. It allowed just a single touchdown. But when it traveled south to Beloit, the outcome was different. Beloit fans flooded the field when the Packers had the ball. One tripped a player headed toward the end zone. The hometown referee waved off three Green Bay touchdowns. The Packers lost, 6–0.

In 1921, the Packers joined the American Professional Football Association (APFA). That league became the National Football League (NFL) in 1922. The Packers did well. Lambeau was a smart and disciplined leader. He was the first professional coach to use the forward pass as a major part of his offense. "Curly was always ahead of his time," noted running back Johnny "Blood" McNally, an early Packers star. "He was always thinking of ways to get an edge." But the Packers had financial problems. In 1923, Lambeau sought help to keep the team afloat. Andrew B. Turnbull, owner of the *Press-Gazette*, persuaded local businessmen to purchase stock in the team. They formed the Green Bay Football Corporation. Most teams have a single primary owner. But the Packers' unique ownership status continues to this day.

LEFT: END BILLY HOWTON

DON HUTSON
END, DEFENSIVE BACK

PACKERS SEASONS: 1935–45
HEIGHT: 6-FOOT-1
WEIGHT: 183 POUNDS

GRIDIRON GREATS v
DON-OF-ALL-TRADES

Don Hutson was one of the most versatile players to ever lace up football cleats. He caught passes on offense as a receiver. He intercepted passes as a defensive back. He made tackles as a defensive end. He kicked extra points, too. In a single quarter of a 1945 game, Hutson scored an astounding 29 points. He caught four touchdown passes and kicked five extra points. He developed many of the passing routes used today. Hutson was a relentless worker. "For every pass I caught in a game," he once said, "I caught a thousand in practice."

CURLY LAMBEAU

"CURLY WAS ALWAYS AHEAD OF HIS TIME. HE WAS ALWAYS THINKING OF WAYS TO GET AN EDGE."

—JOHNNY BLOOD ON CURLY LAMBEAU

In 1929, Lambeau led the Packers to a 12–0–1 record. That earned the team its first NFL championship. Green Bay captured two more titles in 1930 and 1931. In 1933, the Packers endured their first losing season. But then Lambeau signed a young end from the University of Alabama. His name was Don Hutson. He helped propel the Packers to championships in 1936, 1939, and 1944. Sure-handed and speedy, he caught 99 touchdown passes in his career. It was an NFL record that stood for 44 years.

Hutson retired after the 1945 season. Without him, the Packers fell from contention. After the 1949 season, Lambeau stepped down as coach. Quarterback Tobin Rote and right end Billy Howton had some great seasons in the 1950s. But the team struggled. In 1958, the once-proud Packers hit bottom. They won just one game.

GREEN BAY PACKERS

13

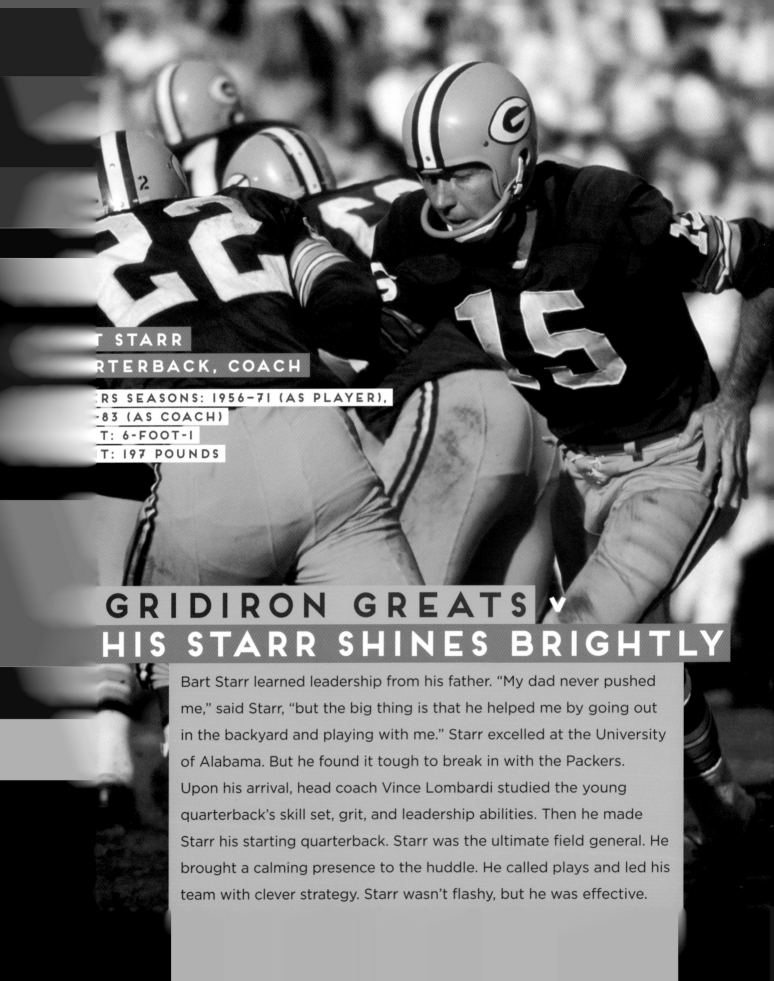

T STARR
RTERBACK, COACH
RS SEASONS: 1956–71 (AS PLAYER),
–83 (AS COACH)
T: 6-FOOT-1
T: 197 POUNDS

GRIDIRON GREATS ∨
HIS STARR SHINES BRIGHTLY

Bart Starr learned leadership from his father. "My dad never pushed me," said Starr, "but the big thing is that he helped me by going out in the backyard and playing with me." Starr excelled at the University of Alabama. But he found it tough to break in with the Packers. Upon his arrival, head coach Vince Lombardi studied the young quarterback's skill set, grit, and leadership abilities. Then he made Starr his starting quarterback. Starr was the ultimate field general. He brought a calming presence to the huddle. He called plays and led his team with clever strategy. Starr wasn't flashy, but he was effective.

167 CAREER TOUCHDOWNS

196 GAMES PLAYED

LOMBARDI COMES TO LAMBEAU

Desperate to improve, the Packers hired Vince Lombardi in 1959. He was a little-known offensive coach from the New York Giants. Lombardi also became Green Bay's general manager. He wanted to revive the Packers through hard work and discipline. He assembled the team. He made it clear that things were going to change. "Gentlemen, I have never been part of a losing team," he announced, "and I do not intend to start now."

Timing was on Lombardi's side. The team already had a core of talented young players. Lombardi coaxed greatness out of them. The offense included halfback Paul Hornung, fullback Jim Taylor, quarterback Bart Starr, and tackle

96

96 CAREER WINS

136

136 GAMES COACHED

GRIDIRON GREATS
ALWAYS A WINNER

"Confidence is contagious. So is lack of confidence." "The only place success comes before work is in the dictionary." "Winning isn't everything—it's the only thing." Vince Lombardi was as quotable as they come. The Packers were a mess when he arrived. But they finished 7-5 in Lombardi's first season. Green Bay went on to win five titles in the next eight seasons, including the first two Super Bowls. Lombardi never had a losing season. The league continues to honor him by awarding the Vince Lombardi Trophy to the Super Bowl winner.

GREEN BAY PACKERS

Forrest Gregg. They would all eventually be enshrined in the Hall of Fame, along with linebacker Ray Nitschke and defensive backs Willie Wood and Herb Adderley.

In 1960, the Packers reached the NFL championship. But they came up short against the Philadelphia Eagles. The next year, they stormed to the title game again. They shut out the Giants, 37–0. "The Pack" dominated the 1962 season. They lost just one game. They held opponents to fewer than eight points seven times during the regular season. In the championship game, the Packers again toppled the Giants. It was their eighth NFL championship. Fans gave their community a new nickname: "Titletown, U.S.A."

Lambeau died before the 1965 season. The team's stadium was renamed Lambeau Field in his honor. With Starr handing the ball off to Hornung and Taylor and throwing it to receiver Carroll Dale, the Packers captured yet another NFL championship. They defeated the Cleveland Browns, 23–12. "Sometimes I wondered if Bart wasn't a machine," guard Jerry Kramer said. "It seemed like he never made a mistake, never showed any pain, and never missed an open receiver."

Before the 1966 season, the NFL and the rival American Football League (AFL) agreed to play a joint championship game. The Packers captured the NFL title. Then they faced the AFL champion Kansas City Chiefs. This game became known as Super Bowl I. During the game, Starr threw two touchdown passes to end Max McGee. Taylor added another touchdown, and halfback Elijah Pitts scored two

VINCE LOMBARDI

"THAT WAS A GAME OF GUTS. OTHER TEAMS WOULD HAVE QUIT IN THAT COLD. WE DIDN'T."

—HENRY JORDAN ON THE ICE BOWL

more. Green Bay whipped the Chiefs, 35–10.

The following year, the Packers took yet another NFL title. This time, they defeated the Dallas Cowboys. The game became known as the "Ice Bowl." The temperature was -13 °F (-25 °C). Windchills were as low as -23 °F (-30.6 °C). The field was a sheet of ice. The referees' metal whistles froze to their lips. They had to end plays by shouting. Green Bay trailed by three with seconds left in the game. The Packers were on the Cowboys' 1-yard line. Starr dove into the end zone. His touchdown clinched the championship. "That was a game of guts," said defensive tackle Henry Jordan. "Other teams would have quit in that cold. We didn't." Two weeks later, Green Bay thrashed the Oakland Raiders in the Super Bowl. The win marked the second time the Packers had won three straight championships. No other franchise had done that even once.

JIM TAYLOR

LEAN YEARS

Super Bowl II was also Lombardi's last game as coach. After nine seasons, he was exhausted. He handed the reins to his assistant, Phil Bengtson. The Packers went just 6–7–1. They missed the playoffs. Their dynasty had ended. Still, "Packer Backers" enjoyed great performances. Fullback John Brockington, wide receiver James Lofton, and quarterback Don "Magic Man" Majkowski were fan favorites during the 1970s and '80s. But victories were hard to come by.

GRIDIRON GREATS v
CHEESY FASHION

Wisconsin is the top producer of the nation's cheese. In the late 1980s, Chicago sports fans referred to Wisconsin sports fans as "Cheeseheads." The term was meant as an insult. But Wisconsinite Ralph Bruno took it as a compliment. In 1987, he cut a foam wedge out of his mother's couch cushion. Then he burned black holes in it. He painted it yellow. He wore it on his head to a game. Soon, he founded Foamation, Inc. to sell his hats to the masses. Today, many sports fans associate Cheesehead hats with Packer fans. They proudly wear their cheesy golden hats far and wide.

98

98 NFL SEASONS AS OF 2018

13

13 CHAMPIONSHIPS AS OF 2018

From 1968 to 1991, the Packers posted just five winning seasons. Bringing in former legendary players to coach didn't help. Bart Starr went 52–76–3 as head coach from 1975 to 1983. Over the next four seasons, Forrest Gregg went 25–37–1. Seeking a revival, the Packers hired Mike Holmgren in 1992. Holmgren had been an assistant coach with the San Francisco 49ers. He had a reputation as one of the game's top offensive strategists. "Mike was a winner, and his attitude rubbed off on us immediately," said wide receiver Sterling Sharpe. Sharpe was one of the team's stars in the early 1990s. He was also a centerpiece of Holmgren's rebuilding plan.

Holmgren looked to young quarterback Brett Favre to rebuild that pride. Favre had come to the Packers from the Atlanta Falcons. Atlanta thought he was too undisciplined. But Holmgren saw a promising player. Favre had a strong arm. He displayed a gift for pulling great plays out of thin air. The Packers struggled to 3–6 under Holmgren. Then they shot off six wins in a row. A loss to the Minnesota Vikings kept them out of the playoffs.

BRETT FAVRE

GRIDIRON GREATS
A MULTITUDE OF OWNERS

Most professional sports teams feature a single prominent owner. Often, the owner is an older, wealthy individual. This is not the case in Green Bay. In 1923, Packers founder Curly Lambeau fell into serious debt. Since then, the organization has been the property of a growing number of owners. They come from all 50 states, Guam, and the U.S. Virgin Islands. Today, Packers, Inc. consists of approximately 4.7 million shares of stock. No individual can own more than 200,000 shares. This keeps anyone from controlling a majority of the franchise. The shareholders meet once a year at Lambeau Field to discuss the best interests of the team.

A key in the Packers' comeback was Reggie White. He joined the team before the 1993 season. White was widely recognized as the league's best defensive lineman. When he arrived in Green Bay, he had already been selected to the Pro Bowl seven times. The Packers were ready for another run at glory.

FAVRE BECOMES A FAVORITE

Favre and White led Green Bay to the playoffs in 1993, 1994, and 1995. Each time, the team fell to its old rival: the Dallas Cowboys. In 1996, though, there was no denying the Pack. Favre threw 39 touchdown passes. The team finished with a franchise-best 13–3 record. Favre led Green Bay to Super Bowl XXXI. It faced the New England Patriots for the title. Favre threw two touchdown passes. White had three sacks. A 99-yard kickoff return by Desmond Howard sealed the 35–21 victory. "It's great to bring a championship back to this town," Favre said. "Our fans deserve this."

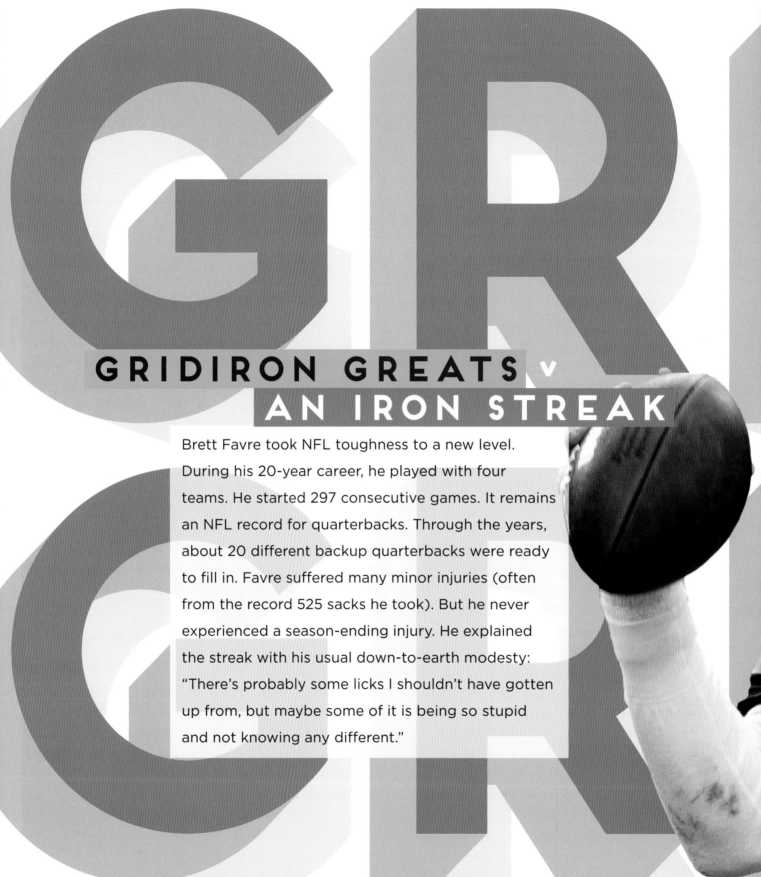

GRIDIRON GREATS v
AN IRON STREAK

Brett Favre took NFL toughness to a new level. During his 20-year career, he played with four teams. He started 297 consecutive games. It remains an NFL record for quarterbacks. Through the years, about 20 different backup quarterbacks were ready to fill in. Favre suffered many minor injuries (often from the record 525 sacks he took). But he never experienced a season-ending injury. He explained the streak with his usual down-to-earth modesty: "There's probably some licks I shouldn't have gotten up from, but maybe some of it is being so stupid and not knowing any different."

BRETT FAVRE
QUARTERBACK

PACKERS SEASONS: 1992–2007
HEIGHT: 6-FOOT-2
WEIGHT: 225 POUNDS

GREEN BAY PACKERS

39

In 1997, Favre was named the NFL's Most Valuable Player (MVP) for the third year in a row. Green Bay returned to the Super Bowl. It was heavily favored to win. But it came up short, losing 31–24 to the Denver Broncos. Green Bay remained a contender for many years. Favre continued to break NFL records.

Green Bay posted 12–4 records in 2001 and 2002. It fell in the playoffs both times. In 2003, the Packers went 10–6. They topped the National Football Conference (NFC) North Division. The Wild Card game against the Seattle Seahawks—now coached by Holmgren—ended in a wild win. Cornerback Al Harris intercepted the ball in overtime. He returned it 52 yards for the winning touchdown. Green Bay lost to the Eagles the following week.

The Pack again took its division in 2004. The playoffs ended bitterly, though. The Vikings beat the Packers at Lambeau Field, 31–17. The loss deflated Green Bay. It slipped to 4–12 in 2005. Some wondered whether Favre had lost his touch. That year, he led the league with 29 interceptions. He completed just 20 touchdown passes.

In 2006, Green Bay hired Mike McCarthy as head coach. He infused the team with new energy. McCarthy helped Favre find success in 2007. At age 38, Favre led the team to a surprising 13–3 record. He set several NFL career passing records along the way: attempts (8,758), completions (5,377), yards (61,655), and touchdowns (442). The Packers opened the playoffs with a 42–20 victory over the Seahawks. Then the Giants came to Lambeau for the NFC Championship Game. The bitterly cold contest went to overtime. The magical season quickly ended. Favre threw an interception. It led to a game-winning field goal by the Giants.

WIDE RECEIVER DONALD DRIVER

MR. RODGERS'S
NEIGHBORHOOD

Shortly afterward, Favre announced his retirement. His replacement was Aaron Rodgers. Rodgers had served as Favre's backup for three years. He displayed Favre-like intensity under pressure. Players such as wide receivers Donald Driver and Greg Jennings, as well as cornerback Charles Woodson and linebacker A. J. Hawk, helped Rodgers succeed. He threw for 4,038 yards and 28 touchdowns in his first season at the helm. But the Packers won only six games.

Rodgers soon made fans almost forget about Favre. The Packers' 11–5 record in 2009 sent them to the playoffs. They lost in overtime to the Arizona Cardinals, 51–45. It was the highest-scoring playoff game

43

in NFL history. Green Bay returned to the postseason in 2010. Despite playing all three games on the road, the Packers fought their way to Super Bowl XLV. Rodgers made three touchdown passes. The Packers defeated the Pittsburgh Steelers, 31–25. "We put everything on his [Rodgers's] shoulders," McCarthy said. "He did a lot at the line of scrimmage for us against a great defense."

Returning the Lombardi Trophy to Titletown brought out the best in the Packers. They started 2011 with 13 straight wins. They finished with a 15–1 record. Rodgers was the season's MVP. But the Giants dashed Green Bay's hope for a Super Bowl repeat in the divisional round. Still, the Packers continued to perform at a high level. They topped the NFC North again in 2012. But they fell to the 49ers in the playoffs. The Pack started strong in 2013. Then, in Week 9, Rodgers suffered a broken collarbone. In his absence, Green Bay struggled. He returned for the final game of the season. His last-minute touchdown pass nudged the Packers into the playoffs. Once again, the 49ers knocked them out. The following year, Rodgers earned MVP honors again as he led the Pack to a 12–4 finish. The team met Seattle in the conference championship. The Seahawks staged an improbable comeback. They emerged from overtime with a 28–22 win.

The Packers lost in overtime again in the 2015 playoffs. In 2016, they returned to the playoffs. But Atlanta cruised to a 44–21 victory in the NFC Championship Game. Green

LEFT: LINEBACKER CLAY MATTHEWS

AARON RODGERS

LINEBACKER BLAKE MARTINEZ

Bay began 2017 with four wins in its first five games. Then Rodgers suffered a fractured collarbone against the Vikings. This time, there was no miracle comeback. The Packers finished 7–9. They were out of the playoffs for the first time in nine years. Green Bay continued to struggle in 2018. It dropped to 6–9–1. Hoping to turn things around, the Packers hired Matt LaFleur as their new head coach for 2019.

During its long history, Green Bay has proven that it can hold its own against the league's big cities. As the Packers continue to work toward their next championship, fans will continue to pack the stands of historic Lambeau Field to cheer them on.

NFL CHAMPIONSHIPS

1929, 1930, 1931, 1936, 1939, 1944, 1961, 1962, 1965, 1966, 1967, 1996, 2010

WEBSITES

GREEN BAY PACKERS

https://www.packers.com/

NFL: GREEN BAY PACKERS TEAM PAGE

http://www.nfl.com/teams/greenbaypackers/profile?team=GB

INDEX

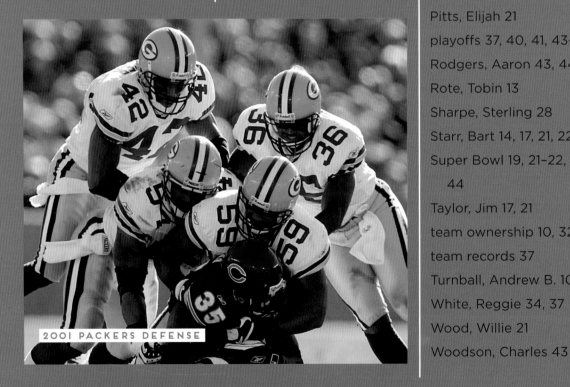

2001 PACKERS DEFENSE